AN IDEAS INTO ACTION GUIDEBOOK

Managing Conflict with Your Boss

Shavan,

Best wishes

Ashav

2/16/05

IDEAS INTO ACTION GUIDEBOOKS

Aimed at managers and executives who are concerned with their own and others' development, each guidebook in this series gives specific advice on how to complete a developmental task or solve a leadership problem.

LEAD CONTRIBUTORS	Davida Sharpe
	Elinor Johnson
CONTRIBUTORS	Talula Cartwright
	Daryl Anne Kline
	Barbara Popejoy
	Ellen Van Velsor
GUIDEBOOK ADVISORY GROUP	Victoria A. Guthrie
	Cynthia D. McCauley
DIRECTOR OF PUBLICATIONS	Martin Wilcox
EDITOR	Peter Scisco
WRITER	Robert Bixby
DESIGN AND LAYOUT	Joanne Ferguson
CONTRIBUTING ARTIST	Laura J. Gibson

CCL No. 416
ISBN No. 1-882197-70-4

CENTER FOR CREATIVE LEADERSHIP
POST OFFICE BOX 26300
GREENSBORO, NORTH CAROLINA 27438-6300
336-288-7210

AN IDEAS INTO ACTION GUIDEBOOK

Managing Conflict with Your Boss

Davida Sharpe and Elinor Johnson

Center for
Creative Leadership

leadership. learning. life.

THE IDEAS INTO ACTION GUIDEBOOK SERIES

This series of guidebooks draws on the practical knowledge that the Center for Creative Leadership (CCL) has generated in the course of more than thirty years of research and educational activity conducted in partnership with hundreds of thousands of managers and executives. Much of this knowledge is shared – in a way that is distinct from the typical university department, professional association, or consultancy. CCL is not simply a collection of individual experts, although the individual credentials of its staff are impressive; rather it is a community, with its members holding certain principles in common and working together to understand and generate practical responses to today's leadership and organizational challenges.

The purpose of the series is to provide managers with specific advice on how to complete a developmental task or solve a leadership challenge. In doing that the series carries out CCL's mission to advance the understanding, practice, and development of leadership for the benefit of society worldwide. We think you will find the Ideas Into Action Guidebooks an important addition to your leadership toolkit.

Other guidebooks currently available:
- *Ongoing Feedback: How to Get It, How to Use It*
- *Becoming a More Versatile Learner*
- *Reaching Your Development Goals*
- *Giving Feedback to Subordinates*
- *Three Keys to Development: Defining and Meeting Your Leadership Challenges*
- *Feedback That Works: How to Build and Deliver Your Message*
- *Communicating Across Cultures*
- *Learning from Life: Turning Life's Lessons into Leadership Experience*
- *Keeping Your Career on Track: Twenty Success Strategies*
- *Preparing for Development: Making the Most of Formal Leadership Programs*
- *Choosing an Executive Coach*
- *Setting Your Development Goals: Start with Your Values*
- *Do You Really Need a Team?*
- *Building Resiliency: How to Thrive in Times of Change*
- *How to Form a Team: Five Keys to High Performance*
- *Using Your Executive Coach*

Table of Contents

EXECUTIVE BRIEF

As individuals, we can be creative and ambitious in our personal lives and in our professional lives. But individual efforts can't always match the energy and productivity of a group. Cultures, societies, clubs, schools, and militaries arose out of our need to band together for mutual support. Organizations were created to deal more effectively with the environment – both the natural world and the world of work. But there is a trade-off when we move from individual contributions to group efforts: the relationships necessary for working together can spawn conflict.

In organizations, tensions between individuals need to be defused, or focused in order to find productive solutions to problems. This is especially critical when conflict arises between people at different levels in the organization, such as when you are having a conflict with your boss. These tensions aren't easy to handle. Conflict can generate discomfort, anger, and ineffective behavior. Feelings such as fear and resentment can rise to the surface. Organizational issues such as unclear lines of authority, power, politics, and ineffective support systems also come into play.

Although these internal and external factors create a rich and complicated landscape for conflict to flourish, a conflict with your boss doesn't necessarily spell the end of your career with an organization. There are steps you can take to gain perspective on conflict and to manage the conflict so that it focuses your energy and your boss's energy on the needs of the organization, moving both of you toward a more productive working relationship.

What Is Conflict?

The word *conflict* is often used to describe a wide range of disagreements – everything from minor squabbles to dysfunctional relationships to all-out war. At its core, conflict is disharmony, dissension, division, and discord between people, interests, or ideas. Conflict is also natural, and inherent to the human experience. Where there are people, there will be conflict.

Individuals perceive conflict differently, and those differences can make managing conflict extremely difficult. What to one person is a full-scale battle to another person is an opportunity to discuss divergent views. One person may define a poor relationship as conflict, but someone else may see the same relationship as difficult but not unusual – just what's expected when working with people who hold different perspectives. These disparate views about conflict can be even more disconcerting when the conflict is between you and your boss.

Why Managing Conflict Is Important

Since 1983 the Center for Creative Leadership has conducted research on derailment – contrasting those people who make it to the top with people who were once successful but in the end were demoted, fired, or sidelined. In the research, successful managers were described as those who seek out, build, and maintain effective relationships with others. They listen – willingly, actively, and patiently. They willingly receive feedback and effectively respond to it. They support others' ideas. They perform as promised and

7

The Look of Conflict

In a large manufacturing company, the vice president of operations had ten direct reports. She got along well with eight of the ten. Two of her reports, however, proved difficult to work with. From her perspective, she felt they were threatened by the changes she had instituted since taking her position because both employees were "old timers." She also knew that they socialized together, and she thought this tended to encourage their mutual negativity. Despite the difficulties, she didn't regard her interactions with these two reports as a "conflict" situation. In her mind, conflicts resulted from personality clashes, not employee resistance. In this case she saw her direct reports as resisting change, and she saw herself as responsible for gaining their commitment.

The two direct reports, the director of quality and the director of manufacturing, described their relationship with the vice president as conflicted. From their perspective, every time they tried to disagree with their less experienced boss, she shut them down. They felt very frustrated. They thought they had tried to get through to her on numerous occasions, and had even talked about how unreceptive she was to their ideas. Because they saw the relationship as filled with conflict, they put more time and emotional energy into fixing the relationship than their boss did. This inequity caused even greater frustration and eventually stopped communication up the chain from director to vice president.

The difference in how the vice president and the directors defined conflict and how they saw their relationship exacerbated all of these problems. Often how individuals define conflict influences how they approach such a relationship. At the same time, each person in the relationship judges that approach based on his or her own view of conflict.

maintain commitments. Derailed managers were described as disconnected, disagreeable, dictatorial, and divisive. They mishandled interpersonal relationships. Specific examples of their ineffective relationships include having an unresolved interpersonal conflict with a boss and showing unprofessional behavior related to a disagreement with upper management.

Conflict with your boss doesn't have to lead to derailment if you make the effort to effectively manage the situation. When you appropriately manage conflict, positive consequences can result. It can lead to a more productive working relationship between you and your boss that:

Increases effort. In many ways, we need our differences to help us clarify our own positions and better understand others. The chaos and confusion that naturally surrounds a search for clarity can actually energize the efforts of all.

Airs feelings. Instead of allowing resentment to build, feelings are dealt with openly.

Leads to better decision making. More information leads to better decisions, even if during a conflict situation each side hears information it doesn't want to hear.

Exposes key issues. Future conflict is avoided by raising important issues while there is time to address them.

Stimulates critical thinking. Consistently raising (and resolving) disagreements contributes to a thinking organization.

Creates open environments. Understanding and managing conflict robs the situation of its destructive power and builds an environment where ideas are vigorously exchanged.

Stimulates creativity and innovation. Creating an open forum for diverse ideas and perspectives creates space for new ideas and new ways of thinking.

On the contrary, if you mishandle a conflict, it can bring negative consequences. Poor interpersonal skills, such as an inability to manage conflict, aren't the only reason managers derail, but they were the reason cited most often in CCL's research. A mishandled or ignored conflict can have dramatic effects on personal and organizational performance that:

Decreases productivity. Disagreements and clashes rob an otherwise productive relationship of its energy.

Decreases communication. Unmanaged conflict breeds fear and resentment, which makes it more unlikely that people will voice their opinions, views, or ideas.

Increases negative feelings. Clashes create bruised feelings and torn relationships. At worst, the organization may lose valuable individuals who seek other employment.

Increases stress. Conflict takes an emotional and physical toll on the individuals involved.

Decreases cooperation. Organizational units, such as teams or workgroups, may split into factions and cliques, each lobbying its own viewpoint.

Encourages backstabbing. The work environment is poisoned with hidden agendas and back-channel maneuverings.

Managing Conflict with Your Boss

The special case of conflict between a direct report and a boss presents unique challenges. As a manager with responsibilities up and down the organizational chain, recognizing and resolving conflicts with your boss may well define to what degree you can effectively contribute to your organization. A conflict with your boss can arise from several different kinds of situations or opposing perspectives. Here are a few examples that illustrate potential roots of a conflict:

There is no role clarity or alignment. You are not sure about how your work supports your boss's work and how it meets the mission of the organization. You may think you're doing tasks that

---

The Look of Conflict

An executive agrees to take on a new position with greater scope and more responsibility. Initially the boss had promised that a pay increase would go with the new position, but that was delayed due to budget shortfalls. After a year the executive is becoming very frustrated and losing trust in her boss.

Unfilled expectations cause many of the conflicts between direct reports and their bosses. Communication – clear and often and open – is one key to managing and resolving those conflicts.

---

should be on your boss's list. Your boss may think that she or he is doing too much of your work.

You and the boss sit at different vantage points. Depending on the structure of your organization, each of you is accountable to a different measure of performance and to different stakeholders. You and your boss may not pay attention to or respond to the same things because you don't hold the same position in the organization.

You lack confidence in your boss's ability. Several different situations could lead you to this perspective. Perhaps you held the interim position prior to your boss's appointment and then the organization asked you to orient your new boss to the job. Perhaps the skills your boss employs aren't as apparent to you as the skills you have to use to get results in your position.

Your boss lacks confidence in you. Your boss may be looking to you for information, advice, and options, but perceives you to be faltering on all fronts.

You and your boss are mismatched in ethics, values, and integrity. Managing conflict that threatens the organizational good because of mismatched ethics, values, or integrity may require you to seek advice and support from reliable internal HR resources or even external support sources (ranging from coaching to legal advice).

My View of Conflict: A Personal Worksheet

Take some time to consider the following list of questions. Answer them as completely and thoughtfully as you can. You may find it useful to record your answers so that you can return to them from time to time to see if your answers and your view toward conflict have shifted.

How do you define conflict?

How do you think your definition of conflict is similar to or different from how those around you define it?

What experiences shaped your views and attitudes about conflict?

What directions related to handling conflict were you given as a child?

How would you describe your communication strategies when you feel uncomfortable or uneasy? (Think of such actions as raising your voice, withdrawing, making wisecracks, laughing, asking questions, and bombarding others with information.)

What are the triggers that for you ignite a conflict?

What are your own attitudes toward conflict?

How do you behave toward your boss?

Are you engaging in any of the following behaviors?

- **Political maneuvering.** Don't go over your boss's head when conflict occurs. Include your boss when you go up the organizational ladder to address a problem. Don't start looking at your next position. Concentrate on the assignments your boss has given you.

- **Lip service.** All talk and no action is a sure way to increase conflict with your boss. Tell your boss what you'll do and then do it.

- **Loose talk.** Don't undermine your boss; it will come back to haunt you. Support your boss when dealing with peers, direct reports, and staff.

- **Apple-polishing.** Don't go overboard. Understanding and supporting your boss's point of view does not mean abandoning your own ideas or values. Nor should you withhold negative information. Determine when to raise issues in a public forum and when to take them behind closed doors.

- **Disagree disagreeably.** It's healthy to disagree, but don't carry the disagreement out of the meeting. Don't let it infect your relationships or prey on your mind.

You and your boss are mismatched in some other regard. This mismatch can run the gamut from management styles to differences in philosophy, motivation, and personality. You may prefer a more directive approach to leadership, for example. You may prefer more structure, and more direction about how to accomplish goals. Your boss may prefer a less directive approach and give his direct reports more freedom to do their work than you are accustomed to or are comfortable with.

It's important to understand the circumstances under which conflicts between you and your boss can arise. Understanding the context allows you to make a full examination of the conflict so you can work toward a resolution. Before you can effectively manage a conflict with your boss, however, you will need to examine your own definition of conflict, your beliefs about conflict, and your behavior during a conflict situation. Your goal is to understand your responses to specific situations, or "triggers," and your reactions, or "coping strategies," to those situations. Once you understand more clearly how different situations can cause conflict, and how you interact with your boss when conflict arises, you will have a clearer view of your own contribution to a conflict situation.

The next step in learning to manage conflict with your boss is to investigate the expectations you and your boss have of each other. Your boss's expectations regarding performance and your own expectations regarding support and development can indicate a point of conflict. If you can clarify those expectations you will be ready to develop strategies for bridging the gap in your working relationship.

Clarifying Expectations

CCL has found that of all the factors important for success within an organization, there are four that your boss is likely to value most: resourcefulness, doing whatever it takes, being a quick study, and decisiveness. These four factors do the most to shape your boss's evaluation of your performance and to define your boss's expectations of your performance. If you are experiencing conflict with your boss, part of that conflict may stem from your failure to understand or meet your boss's expectations in one or more of these key areas.

Using the Performance Expectation Worksheet on pages 16–17, rate your performance related to each of the four factors CCL has found to be most influential in defining your boss's expectations and evaluations.

The Look of Conflict

The director of the Employee Assistance Program (EAP) for a large telecommunications company operated successfully with much autonomy and authority. This program was popular and the director enjoyed his "loose" relationship with his boss. However, a new boss was promoted to the supervisory position and conflict between that boss and the director began. The new boss, eager to make his mark on his new organization, informed the EAP director that he would no longer be in charge of the program. The new boss put himself in charge, changing the director's role to that of an implementer of the program. Following a series of discussions (some heated), both parties defined what they wanted and expected of each other. This clarification convinced the new boss to restore the original authority to the director.

Conflict between a manager and a boss can result from problems related to performance and from mismatches between personality and approaches (or style). When it comes to managing conflict related to performance, your first step is to define your boss's perception of your performance.

Performance Expectation Worksheet

Darken the circle that best describes your own assessment of your performance. After completing the worksheet, examine your answers. What do they say about your strengths and developmental needs? What effect do your strengths and developmental needs have on your behavior toward your boss? Do you behave in ways that might spur conflict, as a way to cover up a developmental need, or as a way to make yourself look better than your boss? What do you think your boss expects of you in each of these areas? [*Suggestion: Give a copy of this assessment to your boss for his or her feedback.*]

Resourcefulness
I can think strategically under pressure

I need to develop this skill.   This is one of my strengths.

O   O   O   O   O   O   O

I can set up complex work systems.

I need to develop this skill.   This is one of my strengths.

O   O   O   O   O   O   O

I exhibit flexible problem-solving behavior.

I need to develop this skill.   This is one of my strengths.

O   O   O   O   O   O   O

I work effectively with higher management in dealing with the complexities of the job.

I need to develop this skill.   This is one of my strengths.

O   O   O   O   O   O   O

Doing whatever it takes
I show perseverance and focus in the face of obstacles.

I need to develop this skill.   This is one of my strengths.

O   O   O   O   O   O   O

I can take charge.

I need to develop this skill.   This is one of my strengths.
○   ○   ○   ○   ○   ○   ○

I can learn from others when necessary.

I need to develop this skill.   This is one of my strengths.
○   ○   ○   ○   ○   ○   ○

Being a quick study
I am able to master quickly new technical and business knowledge.

I need to develop this skill.   This is one of my strengths.
○   ○   ○   ○   ○   ○   ○

Decisiveness
I can make good decisions under pressure.

I need to develop this skill.   This is one of my strengths.
○   ○   ○   ○   ○   ○   ○

I can make decisions and take action in a timely fashion.

I need to develop this skill.   This is one of my strengths.
○   ○   ○   ○   ○   ○   ○

I follow through on decisions.

I need to develop this skill.   This is one of my strengths.
○   ○   ○   ○   ○   ○   ○

If your boss's evaluation doesn't agree with your opinion of yourself, conflict is likely to occur. But finding out what your boss expects of you and understanding his or her perspective isn't so easy. Bosses vary widely in their ability to communicate goals to their direct reports. Therefore, if you have not already, you should take steps to identify your boss's expectations, to review examples of how your boss will know when expectations are being met, and to seek direction for achieving those expectations. Here are a few strategies you can use to gather that kind of information:

Get feedback. Ask for formal and informal feedback through assessment instruments and face-to-face meetings. Use the four factors detailed in the Performance Expectation Worksheet as a reference point for understanding your boss's expectations.

Look around and across your organization. Who gets the resources in your organization? Who gets promoted? Who is rewarded in other ways? What are these individuals doing? What characteristics differentiate your performance from theirs?

Look up in your organization. What does your boss's boss expect? The answer says a lot about what is expected of you.

Uncover the history. Ask other people who report directly to your boss and people who previously reported to your boss what they think is or was expected of them. Review old memoranda and reflect on how projects were launched, carried out, and concluded.

The Look of Conflict

An executive in charge of a major initiative needs the support of his boss to execute the change. During their meetings, the boss asks many questions. From his perspective, the boss believes that by pushing back and playing the devil's advocate he is preparing his direct report for the resistance that's likely to accompany the changes to come. But because the boss wasn't explicit about his "coaching" tactics, the direct report interprets the behavior as unsupportive, even antagonistic – and contemplates resigning.

If you don't understand your boss's behavior in a given situation, give your boss feedback so that you can both be clear on the strategies and tactics being employed for business and developmental purposes.

Mapping Expectations

Think about a situation in which you felt that your boss did not communicate goals to you effectively but still held you accountable for meeting those goals. Describe the situation in the space provided (use a separate sheet of paper if you prefer, leaving ample room for a paragraph on the right side). Don't record information unless you have performed the action listed. If any of the actions are difficult for you to carry out (see page 18), that may indicate you have a developmental need in that area. Not only will you improve your ability to manage conflict by developing acumen in these communication and observation skills, but you will also add to your store of leadership competencies from which you can draw as you move forward in your career.

Situation	
Get Feedback	
Look Around	
Look Up and Down	
Uncover the History	

What does your information tell you? Based on what you've observed, learned, and recorded, can you make assumptions about what your boss expects of you? How do you think your boss viewed the situation? How did your boss respond to the situation? How do those assumptions compare to your assessment of your performance? Is there a gap? Might this gap be the root of your conflict? Has it caused conflict in the past? Might it cause conflict in the future? What factors might have influenced the conflict (both personal and organizational)?

In addition to performance-related expectations, your boss may also have expectations related to your style and approach. If you behave in ways that go against those expectations, conflict can result. Following are some common expectations that bosses have in regard to the behavior of their direct reports. How do you rate your behavior in these areas? Darken the circle that best matches your assessment.

Loyalty. Support your boss and your boss's agenda in public. Don't just go through the motions. Be part of the team. To what degree do you see yourself as showing loyalty?

○　　　○　　　○　　　○　　　○　　　○　　　○
Low Degree　　　　　　　　　　　　　　　High Degree

Openness. Keep the communication channel open between you and your boss. Make honest requests. Disagree with vigor but respect. Speak without hidden motives. To what degree do you see yourself as showing openness?

○　　　○　　　○　　　○　　　○　　　○　　　○
Low Degree　　　　　　　　　　　　　　　High Degree

Tolerance. Allow your boss to be human. Allow your boss to make mistakes and to be imperfect. Resist the temptation to cast your boss as the villain. To what degree do you think you see yourself as showing tolerance?

○　　　○　　　○　　　○　　　○　　　○　　　○
Low Degree　　　　　　　　　　　　　　　High Degree

Focus. Keep on task. Work together, sharing common goals, marking progress toward mutually beneficial results. To what degree do you see yourself as showing focus?

○　　　○　　　○　　　○　　　○　　　○　　　○
Low Degree　　　　　　　　　　　　　　　High Degree

Sharpening Your View

Once you understand your boss's expectations of your performance, you can begin to review how you see your boss. It's usually the case that individuals lean toward one of two common views located at each extreme of a range of perspectives. Those extremes reflect what can be called a *low conflict* or a *high conflict* view. To grasp in which of these two camps your view falls, think objectively about your boss. Separate yourself as much as you can from any emotional ties related to your boss. Consider your boss only as a position, not as a person you may not like. How do you see that position relative to your own?

Low Conflict Extreme	High Conflict Extreme
You see your boss as having indisputable authority.	You see your boss's authority as illegitimate or undeserved.
You avoid and minimize conflict with your boss. You promise too much and cave in to unreasonable demands.	You are in a constant state of war with your boss. You interpret everything your boss does as a sign that he or she has no faith in your ability to do the job. Your boss seems so removed that you never know what is expected of you. Decisions that affect your work are made without your input.

To work effectively with your boss, you will need to move away from these extremes and work toward a middle ground. To help you accomplish that shift, make sure you understand what you seek from the relationship. Use the Boss Expectation Worksheet on pages 22–23 to help you define your view of a good boss.

Boss Expectation Worksheet

If you want to improve your relationship with your boss and handle conflicts in an effective and fruitful way, it's important for you to clarify what expectations you have of your boss's behavior. Use the spaces provided (or a blank sheet of paper) to record information about the leadership traits your boss displays in your work relationship. Using this information, engage your boss in a conversation regarding the expectations each of you has for the other.

Providing Feedback	
When was the last time your boss gave you feedback about your performance?	
How did you respond to that feedback?	
Was the feedback helpful to you in your development (even if the feedback was negative)?	
How frequently do you and your boss meet to discuss your performance?	

Obtaining Necessary Resources	
Do you have access to the resources you need to accomplish your goals and organizational initiatives? If not, why not?	

Creating a Positive Environment	
Do you feel comfortable discussing problems with your boss?	
If not, how could your boss create a more positive environment?	

Supporting Your Development	
What has your boss done in the last six months to support your professional development?	
What, if anything, do you want your boss to do differently to support your development, and in what developmental areas do you want that support?	

Lessons of Experience

It's possible to work toward a solution for a conflict you're having with your boss but meet obstacles unrelated to performance and expectation issues. Sometimes a conflict management strategy falls short because of differences in personalities and behavioral styles. For that reason, it's a good idea to have more than one approach to the problem. One way to gather additional conflict management strategies is to reflect upon your relationship with your direct reports. Think about how you work with your group and answer the following questions to gain insights into how you might more effectively manage conflict with your boss.

- Do you see similarities in your relationships with your direct reports and the relationship you have with your boss?
- Do conflicts arise between you and your direct reports that are similar to the conflicts that occur between you and your boss?
- What kinds of performance and relationship expectations do your direct reports have for you?
- What kinds of performance and relationship expectations do you have for your direct reports?
- What feedback have your direct reports given you about your leadership style?
- Compare the feedback you have received from your direct reports and the way you would describe your boss's leadership style. What are the differences and what are the similarities?
- What methods or strategies have you used to manage conflict with your direct reports that you might be able to use to manage the conflict with your boss?

Examining how you handle conflict with your direct reports is only one way to gather additional conflict management strategies. Another is to seek advice from trusted colleagues. Ask for feedback. Observe the situations that drive your boss toward certain behaviors. Objectively examine every conflict situation to determine if you are contributing to the conflict so that you can effectively manage the situation.

Another important tactic is to develop your persuasion skills. The ability to clearly explain your point of view and to argue for your conclusions and convictions will go a long way toward addressing and managing conflict with your boss. Persuasive tactics come in different forms, but the most effective share a sense of communication that is thoughtful, clear, and understood by all sides.

Seven Steps toward Managing Conflict

CCL has found a seven-step process valuable in helping managers and executives become more strategic about managing conflict. This process is similar to other problem-solving models, but it emphasizes the importance of self-exploration and discovery as part of the process. CCL often describes conflict as a problem wrapped in emotion. There's a direct link between what we feel and what we think, and both of these aspects affect conflict situations. Often people use words like "emotional" and "rational" to describe these two aspects as if they were the Dr. Jekyll and Mr. Hyde of conflict. But what seem like polar opposites actually represent the paradox of managing conflict – it's not about managing just one or the other but about how to manage both the emo-

Three Keys to Persuasive Communication

The key steps in developing persuasive tactics that suit your leadership style and are effective in delivering your point of view include preparing, focusing, and feedback.

1. *Prepare your message.*
   Clarify your ideas before sharing them. Know where you want to take your message. Outline the key points of your message and stay close to your outline. Identify and use concrete examples. Don't speak in generalities that your boss might interpret in ways you don't intend.

2. *Focus your message.*
   Consider the leadership style of your boss. Review what you have learned and observed about your boss's perspectives and expectations. How can you appeal to your boss's interests? What does your boss need from the conversation? Tailor your message to fit your boss's style and needs. Be aware of nonverbal behavior that can dilute your message or cause misunderstanding.

3. *Seek feedback about your message.*
   Don't assume that just because you understand your message your boss does too. Ask for feedback from your boss. Restate your key points and work toward an agreed understanding of your message. Ask your boss if he or she understands what you are saying or if you need to make it clearer or state it differently.

tional (feeling) and rational (thinking) aspects of conflict. Awareness of both perspectives gives you a more complete view of the conflict situation.

1. **Build personal awareness.** Boosting your awareness helps you to understand why you think/feel the way you do when reacting to a conflict situation. Focus your awareness along two lines. First, be aware of the immediate thought and/or

feeling you have in response to an external action or situation (trigger) that causes you to act as if you were in conflict. Second, clarify and be aware of the actions and reactions (coping strategies) you use to avoid dealing with conflict.

2. **Clarify your conflict view.** Examine your own perception of the conflict. Explore your underlying assumptions regarding your beliefs about the situation. Align your thoughts, feelings, and behaviors with the reality of the situation. Address these five components to prepare for the next step:
   - *Who* – identify with whom you are in conflict.
   - *What* – identify the source of the conflict.
   - *When* – choose a date for meeting the person with whom you are experiencing conflict.
   - *Where* – identify a neutral, nonthreatening location for the meeting.
   - *Why* – remind yourself that what you hope to gain from the meeting isn't a victory but a mutually beneficial solution to the conflict.

3. **Understand the perspective of others.** The capacity to see things from another point of view is essential to managing conflict successfully. To reach this understanding, first manage your own emotions. Then, have a conversation with your boss to obtain his or her point of view. There are three components to understanding the perspective of others: suspend judgment, ask questions to enlarge your perspective, and validate the perspective of others.

4. **Brainstorm solutions.** Look for common ground. Have a discussion with your boss. Establish rapport, express yourself honestly and openly, be specific, and ask for feedback. If conflict arises from differences in values or ideas, finding common ground – even agreeing to disagree – can break the

tension of the conflict cycle. If the conflict is related to a task, multiple solutions may be possible.

5. **Create an action plan.** Make a plan to address the issues you uncovered in step 4. Discuss your action plan with your boss and solicit feedback.

6. **Implement your action plan.** Update your boss on your progress according to the plan you developed and discussed in step 5.

7. **Evaluate your action plan.** To learn how to better manage conflict in the future, review each conflict experience you have and record what worked and what did not in managing the conflict situation. Keeping a personal learning journal can aid you in this process.

There is likely to always be conflict between managers and their bosses. It's almost impossible to avoid, given human nature and the pressures of organizational life. But conflict can be managed so that it's a positive encounter that leaves both sides creatively involved in their work, eager to insert and support their ideas. Conflict, when handled right, can help to create a workplace that is rewarding and invigorating.

Suggested Readings

Bolton, R. (1986). *People skills: How to assert yourself, listen to others, and resolve conflict.* New York: Simon & Schuster.

Borisoff, D., & Victor, D. A. (1997). *Conflict management: A communication skills approach* (2nd ed.). Boston: Allyn & Bacon.

Carlson, R. (1998). *Don't sweat the small stuff at work: Simple ways to minimize stress and conflict while bringing out the best in yourself and others.* New York: Hyperion Books.

Cloke, K., & Goldsmith, J. (2000). *Resolving conflicts at work: A complete guide for everyone on the job.* San Francisco: Jossey-Bass.

Goleman, D. (1998). *Working with emotional intelligence.* New York: Bantam.

Hirsch, S. K., & Kise, J. (1996). *Work it out: Clues for solving people problems at work.* Palo Alto, CA: Davies-Black Publishing.

van Slyke, E. (1999). *Listening to conflict: Finding constructive solutions to workplace disputes.* New York: AMACOM.

Weeks, D. (1992). *The eight essential steps to conflict resolution: Preserving relationships at work, at home, and in the community.* Los Angeles, CA: Jeremy Tarcher.

Weisinger, H. (2000). *Emotional intelligence at work.* San Francisco: Jossey-Bass.

Background

The Center for Creative Leadership's Foundations of Leadership program (FOL) is a three-day activity-enriched experience that teaches the basics of effective leadership. FOL focuses on personal awareness and growth, working relationships, influence skills, and conflict resolution. That last point – conflict resolution – emerged as a key theme during the program's design.

CCL used its extensive experience in educating leaders in the area of personal awareness to develop a way to approach conflict that moved beyond negotiation or tactics. Instead, CCL asked FOL participants to become aware of their thoughts and feelings about conflict, to be aware of the influence that reason and emotion exert during a conflict situation, and to be mindful of those thoughts and feelings as a means of managing conflict so that it enriches working relationships instead of damaging them.

This basic idea, summed up in the phrase "conflict is a problem wrapped in emotion," gave rise to a seven-step process through which managers can approach, navigate, and manage conflict situations. FOL has since undergone revision, but the link to personal awareness as a key element to managing conflict remains intact.

Key Point Summary

When conflict arises between people at different levels in the organization, the path toward resolution can be hard to see. Before you can manage a conflict with your boss, it's important for you to examine your own definition of conflict, your beliefs about conflict, and your behavior during a conflict situation. It also requires you to assess your boss's perception and expectation of your performance.

Your boss may also have expectations related to your style of creating and maintaining effective working relationships. Many bosses have a high regard for loyalty, openness, tolerance, and focus. If you fail to meet those expectations, conflict can result.

Likewise, you should be aware of your own expectations regarding what you need from your boss in terms of performance, support, and feedback. When you understand the expectations on both sides you will have a broader understanding of the landscape on which the conflict rests and be better able to work toward a resolution.

A seven-step conflict management plan includes (1) building your personal awareness, (2) clarifying your view of conflict, (3) understanding the perspective of others, (4) brainstorming a solution, (5) creating an action plan, (6) implementing the action plan, and (7) reflecting on the process to learn what works and what doesn't.

ORDER FORM

To order, complete and return a copy of this form or contact the Center's Publication Area at: Post Office Box 26300 • Greensboro, NC 27438-6300 • Phone 336-545-2810 • Fax 336-282-3284. You can also order via the Center's online bookstore at www.ccl.org/publications

	QUANTITY	SUBTOTAL
❑ I would like to order additional copies of **Managing Conflict with Your Boss** (#416) $8.95 ea.*		
❑ I would like to order other Ideas Into Action Guidebooks.		
❑ **Ongoing Feedback** (#400) $8.95 ea.*		
❑ **Reaching Your Development Goals** (#401) $8.95 ea.*		
❑ **Becoming a More Versatile Learner** (#402) $8.95 ea.*		
❑ **Giving Feedback to Subordinates** (#403) $8.95 ea.*		
❑ **Three Keys to Development** (#404) $8.95 ea.*		
❑ **Feedback That Works** (#405) $8.95 ea.*		
❑ **Communicating Across Cultures** (#406) $8.95 ea.*		
❑ **Learning from Life** (#407) $8.95 ea.*		
❑ **Keeping Your Career on Track** (#408) $8.95 ea.*		
❑ **Preparing for Development** (#409) $8.95 ea.*		
❑ **Choosing an Executive Coach** (#410) $8.95 ea.*		
❑ **Setting Your Development Goals** (#411) $8.95 ea.*		
❑ **Do You Really Need a Team?** (#412) $8.95 ea.*		
❑ **Building Resiliency** (#413) $8.95 ea.*		
❑ **How to Form a Team** (#414) $8.95 ea.*		
❑ **Using Your Executive Coach** (#415) $8.95 ea.*		
❑ **Feedback Package** (#724; includes #400, #403, #405) $17.95 ea.		
❑ **Individual Leadership Development Package** (#726; includes #401, #404, #409, #411) $26.95 ea.		
Add sales tax if resident of CA (7.5%), CO (6%), NC (6.5%)	**SALES TAX**	
U.S. shipping (UPS Ground – $4 for 1st book; $0.95 each additional book) Non-U.S. shipping (Express International – $20 for 1st book; $5 each additional book)	**SHIPPING**	
CCL's Federal Tax ID #23-707-9591	**TOTAL**	

*Single title quantity discounts: 5-99 – $7.95; 100-499 – $6.50; 500+ – $5.95

DISCOUNTS ARE AVAILABLE
IF ORDERING BY MAIL OR FAX, PLEASE COMPLETE INFORMATION BELOW.

PAYMENT

❏ My check or money order is enclosed. **(Prepayment required for orders less than $100.)**

❏ Charge my order, plus shipping, to my credit card.
  ❏ American Express   ❏ Discover   ❏ MasterCard   ❏ Visa

Acct. # _____   Expiration Date: Mo./Yr. _____

Name as appears on card _____

Signature of card holder _____

SHIP TO

Name _____

Title _____

Organization _____

Street Address _____

City/State/Zip _____

Phone (   ) _____
Your telephone number is required for shipping.

❏ **CHECK HERE TO RECEIVE A COMPLETE GUIDE TO CCL PUBLICATIONS.**
❏ **CHECK HERE TO RECEIVE INFORMATION ABOUT CCL PROGRAMS AND PRODUCTS.**

ORDER BY PHONE: 336-545-2810 • ONLINE: WWW.CCL.ORG/PUBLICATIONS